Contents

The giraffe

The giraffe is the tallest animal in the world. It could look into a second-floor window without having to stand on tiptoe! It has an incredibly long neck and four long legs. Each giraffe has its own unique pattern of brown patches on a lighter yellowish background.

bull

cow

A male giraffe is called a bull and a female is called a cow. A young giraffe is called a calf.

FANTASTIC FACT

A bull grows as tall as 5.5 metres. A cow is slightly shorter than a bull at 4.5 metres tall.

ANIMAL LIVES
GIRAFFES

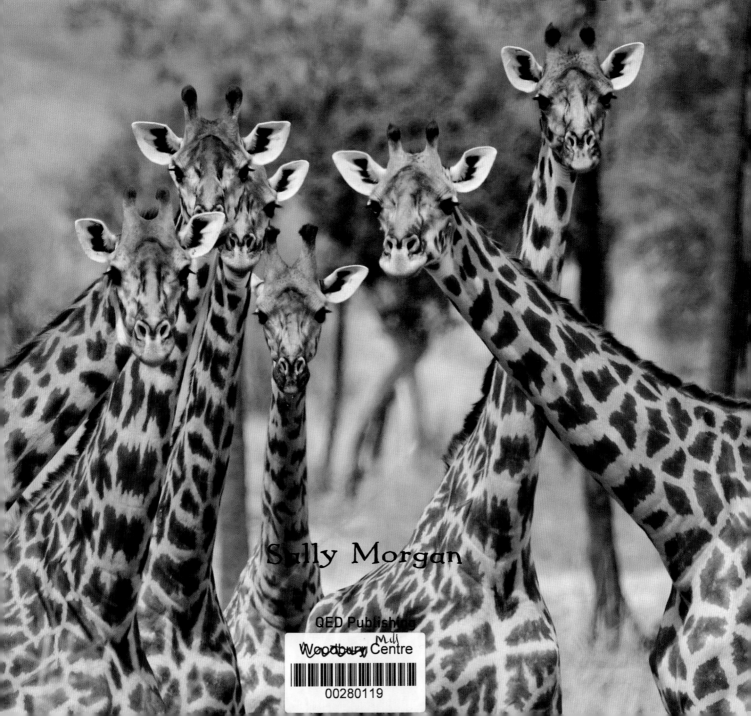

Sally Morgan

QED Publishing

Designed and edited by Calcium

First published in the UK in 2014 by
QED Publishing
A Quarto Group company
The Old Brewery, 6 Blundell Street,
London, N7 9BH

www.qed-publishing.co.uk

A catalogue record for this book is available from the British Library.

ISBN: 978 1 78171 530 7

Printed in China

Photo credits
(t=top, b=bottom, l=left, r=right, c=centre, fc=front cover)

Corbis fc ZSSD/Minden Pictures; **FLPA** 1 Marius Swart/Biosphoto, 2–3 Ingo Arndt/Minden Pictures, 5b Suzi
Eszterhas/Minden Pictures, 8–9 Bernd Zoller/Imagebroker, 9tl Christian Hutter/Imagebroker, 9tc Richard Du Toit/
Minden Pictures, 9b Rolf Schulten/Imagebroker, 10–11 Suzi Eszterhas/Minden Pictures, 11t Marina Horvat/
Imagebroker, 12–13 Konrad Wothe/Minden Pictures, 15t Konrad Wothe/Minden Pictures, 15b Imagebroker, 16-17
Jurgen & Christine Sohns, 18-19 Shin Yoshino/Minden Pictures, 19t Richard Du Toit/Minden Pictures, 19b
Mitsuaki Iwago/Minden Pictures, 20-21 Frans Lanting, 22-23 Imagebroker, 24-25 Richard Du Toit/Minden Pictures,
25t Christian Heinrich/Imagebroker, 27t Jean-Jacques Alca/Biosphoto, 28-29 Ingo Arndt/Minden Pictures, 29t Rolf
Schulten/Imagebroker, 32 Rolf Schulten/Imagebroker; **Getty Images** 27b
Jonathan And Angela/The Image Bank; **NHPA** 26-27 Kevin Schafer/
Photoshot; **Shutterstock** 4–5 Jo Hounsom, 5t Mythja, 6–7 Oleg
Znamenskiy, 9tr Riekephotos, 10 Matt Ragen, 13t Daniel Alvarez,
14-15 MattiaATH, 17t Vadim Petrakov, 21r Johan Swanepoel,
30t Henk Bentlage, 30l EcoPrint, 30br Pichugin Dmitry, 31
Mythja, bc(l) Vaclav Volrab, bc(r) Benoit Daoust.

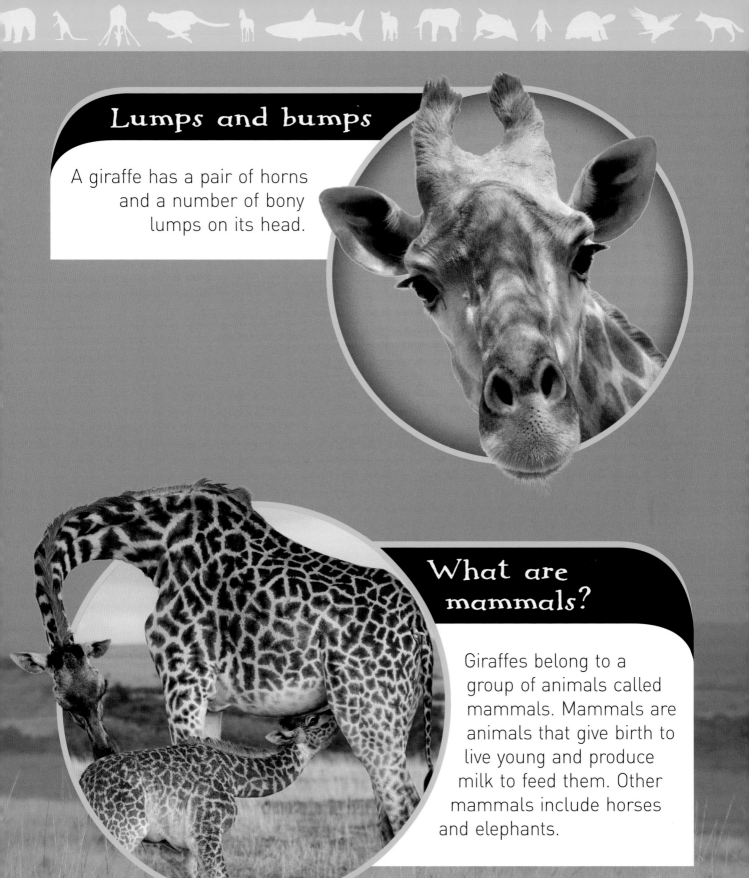

Lumps and bumps

A giraffe has a pair of horns and a number of bony lumps on its head.

What are mammals?

Giraffes belong to a group of animals called mammals. Mammals are animals that give birth to live young and produce milk to feed them. Other mammals include horses and elephants.

Where giraffes live

Giraffes live only in Africa, south of the Sahara Desert. Most live in eastern and southern Africa. Giraffes were once common in drier parts of Africa, too, such as the Sudan, Chad and Ethiopia. Due to hunting, their numbers have declined in these areas.

FANTASTIC FACT

Due to their excellent **camouflage**, giraffes have been mistaken by many people for old, dead trees.

Giraffes live in small groups, called herds. They roam freely across huge areas of savannah such as this one in Africa.

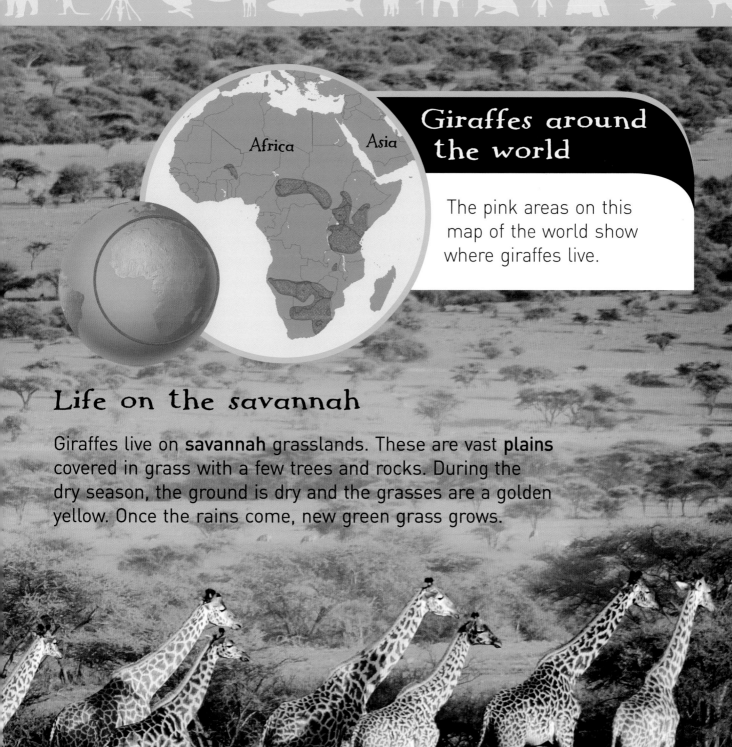

Giraffes around the world

The pink areas on this map of the world show where giraffes live.

Africa

Asia

Life on the savannah

Giraffes live on **savannah** grasslands. These are vast **plains** covered in grass with a few trees and rocks. During the dry season, the ground is dry and the grasses are a golden yellow. Once the rains come, new green grass grows.

Giraffe types

There is only one species, or type, of giraffe. However, there are some small differences between giraffes living in different parts of Africa. For this reason, the giraffe species is divided into nine **subspecies**. Many of these subspecies are named after the areas in which they live. For example, the Masai giraffe is from the Masai Mara in Kenya.

Masai giraffe

The Masai giraffe has a pattern that looks like leaves.

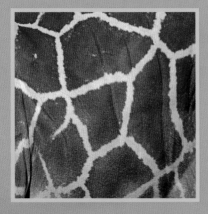

Reticulated giraffe

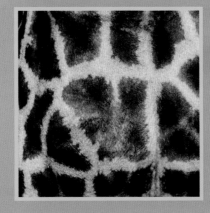

South African giraffe

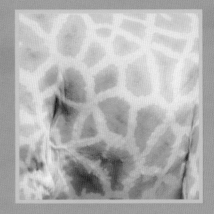

West African giraffe

Coat colours

As well as having different patterns, giraffe coats may vary in colour, too. This is determined by giraffes eating different plants and by where they live. Giraffes that live in drier, dustier places have paler yellow coats because they have **adapted** to their surroundings.

FANTASTIC FACT

People once thought the giraffe was a camel with leopard spots. The giraffe's Latin name, *Giraffa camelopardalis*, means camel–leopard.

Rothschild's giraffe

The Rothschild's giraffe is from Uganda and northern Kenya. It has deep brown, rectangular spots.

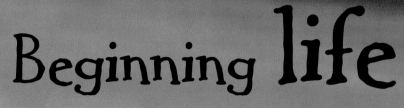

Beginning life

A female giraffe is ready to have her first calf when she is about five years old. After mating, she is **pregnant** for about 15 months. Giraffes give birth to one calf at a time. Twin calves are very rare.

Calves grow quickly, as much as 2 centimetres a day. Some double their height in just one year.

Born tall

A newborn calf weighs about 100 kilograms and is just under 2 metres tall – that's as tall as an adult man!

First drink

As soon as it can stand, the newborn calf takes its first drink of its mother's milk.

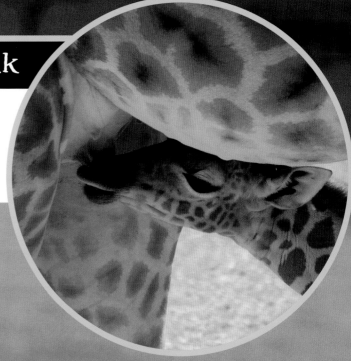

Protective mothers

Giraffes are very protective of their calves and will kick any animal that comes too close. Most giraffe calves are born at the same time of year. This is because more calves survive if they are born together, since **predators** cannot kill all of them.

FANTASTIC FACTS

Giraffes give birth in a place called a calving ground.
. . . .
A female giraffe will often return to where she was born to have her own baby.

Growing up

For the first few days of its life, the calf sits in the grass while its mother goes off to feed. When the calf is one or two weeks old, it is introduced to other giraffes. The calf drinks its mother's milk for 15 to 18 months, although it also eats leaves from about four months of age.

Dangerous days

The first few months after birth are very dangerous for young giraffes. They are hunted by predators, such as hyenas (right), lions, leopards and hunting dogs.

Leaving mum

Young bull giraffes leave their mothers when they are about 15 months old. They join up with other bulls to form an all-male group. Young cow giraffes leave when they are about 18 months old, but they do not go very far and tend to stay in the same area as their mothers.

young calves

Older calves are left in a nursery group while their mothers go to feed. One cow stays behind to care for them.

FANTASTIC FACT

The giraffe has the longest tail of any land mammal. Its tail grows to just under 2.5 metres long!

Living in a herd

Giraffes are sociable animals and live in groups called herds. Herds are made up of individuals of one sex – for example, the cows and their young or a group of young bulls. There are usually between 12 and 15 animals in a herd.

Moving between herds

The individuals in a herd do not stay together all the time. Giraffes wander off and join other herds in the area. However, some giraffes do stay together.

FANTASTIC FACT

It is thought that giraffes sleep for between just 20 minutes and 2 hours in every 24 hours.

Staying together

Giraffes that stay together may be mother and daughter, or unrelated giraffes that are friends.

Living in a herd helps to protect giraffes against predators.

Living alone

The only giraffes that prefer to live alone are older bulls. These giraffes wander over the savannah, looking for cow giraffes.

Home range

Herds of cow giraffes live in a large area that is called a **home range**. However, unlike mammals such as lions, they do not guard the boundaries of their home range. The cows tend to stay in the central part of their home range when looking for food. They get to know this area very well. When giraffes move into the outer parts of their home range, they are more alert because they do not know it as well.

Wanderers

Bull giraffes live either on their own or with other bulls, depending on how old they are. They move through the home ranges of the cows and may travel dozens of kilometres every day. The young bulls are great wanderers and they will travel long distances in only a few months.

Giraffes know where to find food easily on their home range.

FANTASTIC FACT

A giraffe herd drinks and rests in shifts. During shifts, one giraffe remains on the lookout for predators to keep the herd safe.

Feeding

Giraffes are plant-eaters, or **herbivores**. They are **browsing** animals that feed on the leaves of trees. Often, trees have long thorns to stop browsing animals eating their leaves. However, thorns do not stop giraffes! Giraffes pull the leaves and thorns into their mouths. Then they produce lots of saliva to help chew and swallow the thorny mixture.

FANTASTIC FACT

The tongue of the giraffe is about 46 centimetres long. That is as long as a child's arm!

You can tell a bull (above) from a cow by the way it eats. Cows tend to bend their necks, while bulls eat at full stretch.

Other food

As well as leaves and thorns, giraffes also eat flowers, fruits and seeds. Giraffes sometimes even eat bones for their nutrients.

Tongue and lips

Giraffes use their tongue and thick lips to pull leaves into their mouth.

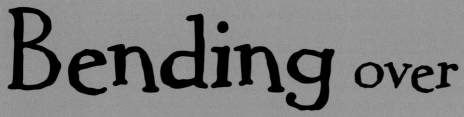

Bending over

Believe it or not, the long neck of the giraffe has the same number of bones as a person's neck – that's just seven **vertebrae**. However, each vertebra of the giraffe is much longer than the vertebra of a human. The heart of a giraffe is very large so it can pump blood all the way up to the head.

There are special **valves** in the blood vessels of the neck that stop blood rushing to the giraffe's head when it bends over.

Kneeling to drink

Giraffes get most of their water from the leaves they eat, but sometimes they have to drink from a river or waterhole. To reach down, they move their front feet apart, bend their knees and lower their necks.

FANTASTIC FACT

The heart of a giraffe weighs 10 kilograms. That is about 25 times heavier than a human heart.

Dangerous thirst

Kneeling to drink is a very dangerous time for giraffes. It is easy for a predator, such as a crocodile, to grab hold of a giraffe when it is bent over.

Senses

Senses are very important to all mammals, and this is also true of giraffes. The giraffe uses its senses to find food, watch for predators and keep an eye on its young.

The giraffe has no trouble seeing over the long grasses and bushes of the savannah.

Super sight

Giraffes have excellent eyesight. One of the advantages of being so tall is that they can see for long distances, too. Their eyes are positioned on the sides of their head, which means that they can see predators creeping up behind them.

By moonlight

Giraffes do not have very good night vision, so they are active only on moonlit nights.

Hearing and smelling

Giraffes' hearing and sense of smell are also good. They can move their ears to follow the direction of a sound. The bulls have a particularly good sense of smell, and this allows them to find cows that are ready to mate.

Movement

Giraffes are **hoofed** mammals, but they walk in a different way from other mammals, such as horses or antelopes.

Unusual mover

Most four-legged mammals walk forward by moving one leg on each side at a time. However, when giraffes walk they swing both legs on one side of their body forward at the same time and then they move the legs on the other side. When giraffes gallop, both back legs are moved forward together, then the front legs are moved forward.

Galloping giraffes can move very quickly over the savannah.

FANTASTIC FACT

Giraffes can gallop at speeds of up to 60 kilometres per hour. Calves can gallop even faster than adult giraffes.

Pacing around

The unusual way in which a giraffe walks is called pacing.

Balancing act

As a giraffe gallops, its heavy head moves forward with each powerful stride, then swings back to help the giraffe balance as it runs.

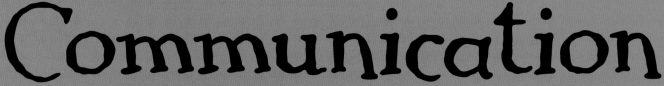

Communication

Giraffes are mostly silent animals, but they can make a variety of sounds. These sounds include grunts, snorts, moans and hisses. A cow looking for her calf will bellow loudly. Sight also plays a role in giraffe communication. This is because they recognize each other from the pattern of their markings.

Calves bleat and make mewing sounds, a bit like a cat.

FANTASTIC FACTS

Some giraffe sounds, called infrasound, cannot be heard by humans.

. . . .

Scientists once thought that giraffes made no sound at all!

Fighting

Very rarely, male giraffes fight to show their strength. Two fighting bulls smash their heads against each other's bodies. Fortunately, the skull of the bull is extra thick, so it is not damaged.

Necking

Young bulls work out their position within a herd by necking. This is when the bulls wrap their necks around each other and push and pull.

Giraffes under threat

Over the last 100 years, the number of giraffes has fallen. Hunting has reduced the number of giraffes living in the northern parts of Africa. There are also very few giraffes left in West Africa. However, in the rest of Africa, giraffes are doing well and their numbers are increasing.

Loss of habitats

Giraffes are also suffering from a loss of their **habitat**. Areas of the savannah are being used to graze sheep and goats. It is also being ploughed up for farmland and built on to create new towns and cities.

Tourists come to see giraffes in their natural habitat, and they bring in valuable money for the local people.

Giraffe future

One way to conserve giraffes is to protect their habitat from disturbance and damage. Areas of savannah can be made into national parks and game reserves.

Life cycle of a giraffe

A cow giraffe is ready to breed when she is five years old. She is pregnant for 15 months and gives birth to a single calf. The calf stays with its mother for about 15 to 18 months. A cow has six or seven calves in her lifetime. Giraffes live up to 25 years in the wild and 28 years in captivity.

newborn calf

older calf

adult

Glossary

adapted when an animal has changed in order to suit the environment in which it lives

browsing when an animal feeds on leaves from trees and shrubs, rather than on grass on the ground

camouflage when an animal blends in with its surroundings

habitat the place in which an animal lives

herbivores animals that eat plants

home range an area where a giraffe spends its life

hoofed having hard coverings over the end of the toes. Mammals, such as horses, giraffes and deer, are hoofed animals

plains large areas of flat land

predators animals that hunt and eat other animals

pregnant when a female animal has a baby or babies developing inside her

savannah a grassy plain found in tropical parts of the world

subspecies groups within a species that look slightly different from each other

valves flaps within blood vessels that stop the blood flowing backward

vertebrae (singular vertebra) the small bones that make up the backbone, including the neck

Index